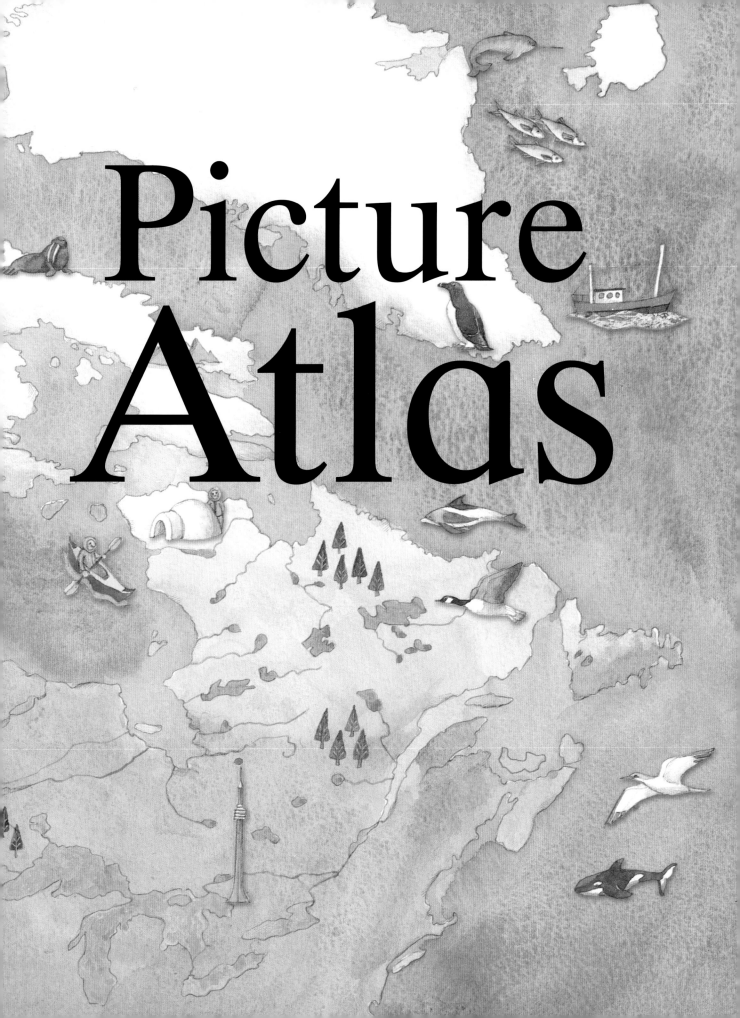

Picture Atlas

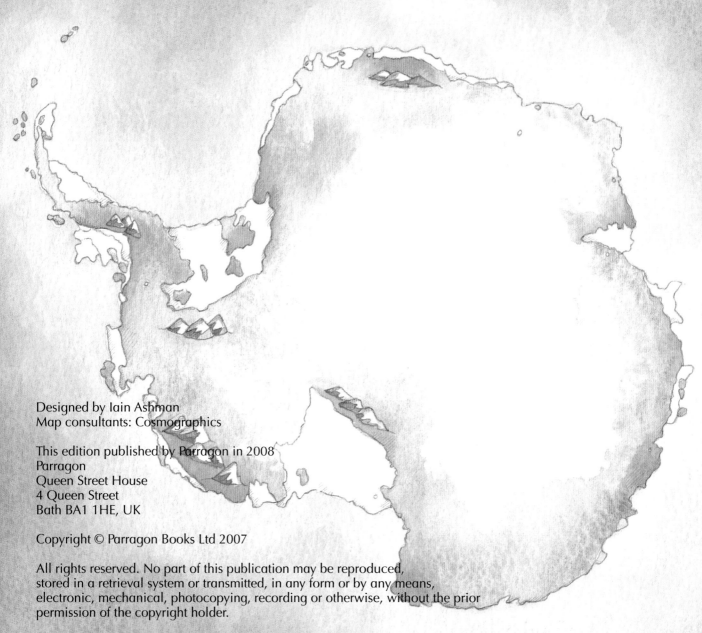

Designed by Iain Ashman
Map consultants: Cosmographics

This edition published by Parragon in 2008
Parragon
Queen Street House
4 Queen Street
Bath BA1 1HE, UK

ISBN 978-1-4075-0143-7

Printed in Indonesia

Gold Stars®

Picture Atlas

Illustrated by Helen Cann

Written by Pamela Beasant

PaRragon

Bath New York Singapore Hong Kong Cologne Delhi Melbourne

Contents

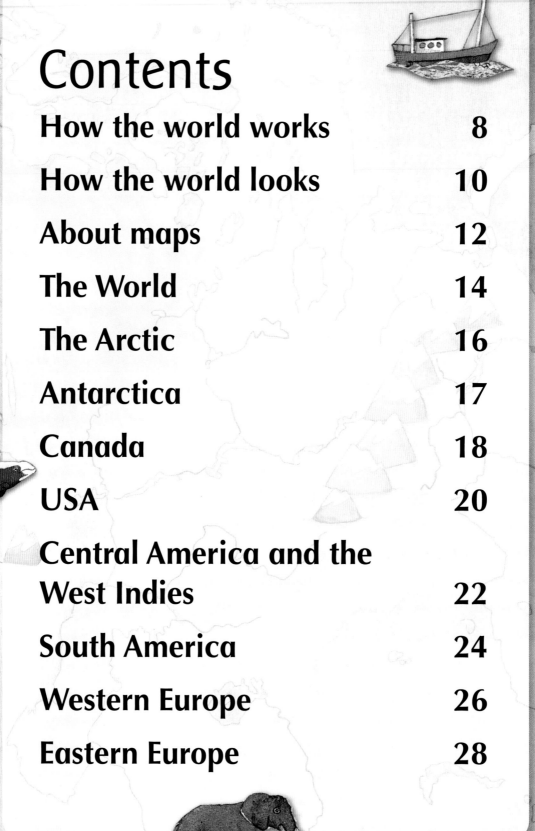

How the world works

Our world is an amazing place! It is the only planet we know about where people, animals and plants can live. We can live here because we have water and sunlight, and can grow food and breathe the air.

What is the world made of?

The world is made mostly of rock. Towards the Earth's centre (called the core) the rock melts because it is so hot. We live on a thin layer of land around the outside, called the crust.

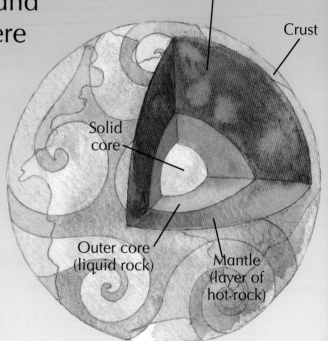

A diagram of how the world looks on the inside.

Crust

Solid core

Outer core (liquid rock)

Mantle (layer of hot rock)

Plates

The Earth's crust is made up of giant pieces of rock called plates. The edges of the plates sometimes move against each other, causing earthquakes. Hot gas and rocks from under the crust sometimes explode through volcanoes.

Earth's crust

Most of the mountains in the world were pushed up millions of years ago when plates crashed together.

Mantle (hot rocks under the crust)

Eruptions and earthquakes happen where two plates meet.

During eruptions hot rock called magma is pushed up from under the Earth's crust. When the magma cools, it forms new land.

8

Hot and cold

The world spins around the Sun. It takes a year to go round once. The hottest parts of the world are nearest the Sun. The coldest parts are at the very top and bottom, at the North and South Poles. They are farthest away from the Sun's heat.

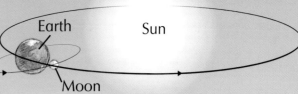

The Earth goes around the Sun, and the Moon goes around the Earth.

Earth   Sun

Moon

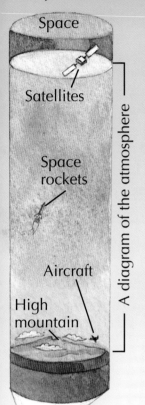

Space

Satellites

A diagram of the atmosphere

Space rockets

Aircraft

High mountain

The atmosphere

Around the Earth there is a layer of air called the atmosphere. It contains the oxygen we need to breathe. As it gets higher, the atmosphere becomes thinner until it disappears and space begins. That is why people who go into space have to take breathing equipment.

The atmosphere

How people live

People can live in most places in the world, but in some areas it is hard to survive. In very hot places, such as deserts, the Sun's heat can kill and there is often not enough to drink. In very chilly places the cold can be dangerous. For instance, people can only survive outside in the Antarctic if they wear lots of protective clothing.

Weather

Weather is caused by the flow of air around the world. Storms happen when the air is moving very quickly. The worst storms are hurricanes – very strong winds that can do lots of damage.

DID YOU KNOW?

The world's water is recycled naturally. Water from the oceans, rivers and lakes rises up (evaporates) into the air. It is carried round the world and falls back to Earth as rain.

How the world looks

The world looks very different depending on where you live. There are high mountains, wide rivers, massive forests, flat plains and huge deserts. Some countries have good farm land, while others have little water and it is hard to grow food there. How people live partly depends on their country's weather and its landscape.

The highest mountains are the Himalayas in Asia.

The longest mountain range is the Andes in South America.

Mountains

Mountains are the highest things on Earth. They have been around for millions of years. A group of mountains in the same area is called a range.

Forests

The world's forests are very important because trees give out the oxygen we need to breathe, and provide us with wood. Tropical rainforests are forests that grow in warm wet areas of the world.

The biggest rainforest is Amazonia, South America.

Rivers

All rivers start small, high up in mountains or hills. As they flow across the land they become deeper and wider. They eventually flow into the sea.

The longest river is the Nile in North Africa.

Deserts

Deserts are huge areas of land that have very little water. Not much can grow in a desert and it is difficult to live there. Most deserts are hot, but some are cold.

Some animals and plants can survive well in deserts.

Desert people called nomads have the skills to live in desert lands.

Grasslands

Some countries have huge areas of flat, open grasslands. In North America this is called prairie. In South America it is the pampas, and in Russia it is called the steppe.

In Africa the grasslands are called the savanna. Lots of wild animals live there.

Countries

The world is divided into seven huge areas called continents. Each continent, (except for Antarctica) has lots of different countries of all shapes and sizes.

The smallest country is Vatican City in Italy.

The biggest country is Russia.

Countries on the same piece of land have borders between them. Borders are shown in red on the maps in this book.

Cities

Most countries have large cities, as well as smaller towns and villages. The main city is called the capital. On the maps in this book, capital cities are shown as blue squares.

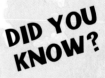

DID YOU KNOW?

There are more than 190 countries, and over 3,000 different languages spoken in the world.

About maps

Maps show what places look like, seen from high above. They show the outline of a country or a town, and as much detail as possible about what the land is like and how it is used. Maps used to be made by people walking around studying the land. Now, photographs from satellites in space are used to make very accurate maps.

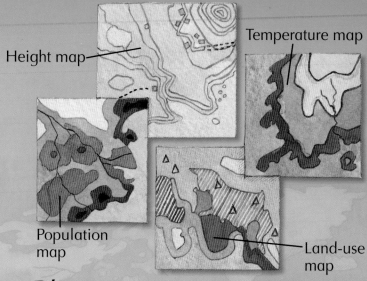

Height map

Temperature map

Population map

Land-use map

Picture maps

Maps can show different things. Some show how hot or cold a place is, or how high the land is. Others show what crops are grown, or how many people live there. The maps in this book are picture maps. They show places of interest, along with mini pictures.

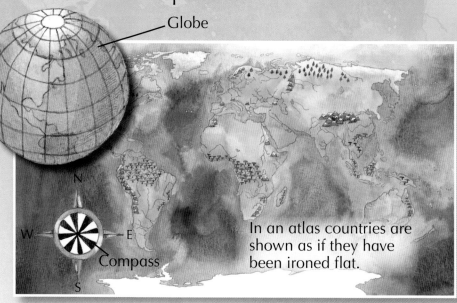

Globe

N

W   E

Compass

S

In an atlas countries are shown as if they have been ironed flat.

Flat world

The world is a ball shape, and the best way to show an accurate map of the world is on a globe. In an atlas, a map of the world shows all the countries as if the world has been rolled out flat. It is not quite as accurate as a globe.

North and south

Most maps have a compass that shows the direction of north, south, east and west. There is a compass on every map in this book.

The Equator

Maps often show an imaginary line running round the middle of the world. This is called the Equator, which divides north from south. The climate near the Equator is much warmer and wetter than it is at the North and South Poles.

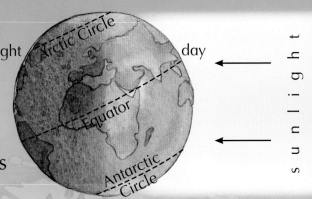

The lines showing the Arctic and Antarctic Circles mark the areas where days and nights last a very long time. For half the year, it is totally light, and for half the year the sun does not rise at all.

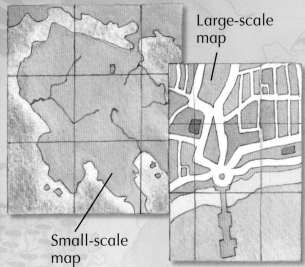

Large-scale map

Small-scale map

Big and small maps

Maps can show huge areas such as the whole world, or a small area such as one town. On a map of the world, a small distance represents many kilometres. Whether a map shows a big or a small area is called its 'scale'.

Map Key

Map-makers use symbols to show things such as mountains and forests. Sometimes they explain what the symbols mean on the map. This is called a key.

The key to some of the symbols used on the maps in this book.	River	Pine forest
City	Lake	Country border
Capital city	Rainforest	Mountains

The World

The oceans surround the land we live on. The Pacific is the biggest and deepest ocean on earth. It covers about a third of the planet.

The seven continents are North America, South America, Asia, Africa, Europe, Australasia and Antarctica. They are outlined on the map here.

Largest island in the world.
Greenland

Alaska

polar bear

NORTH AMERICA

EUROPE

blue whale

ATLANTIC OCEAN

Mediterrane Sea

bald eagle

AFRICA

Hawaii

cruise ship

camels

turtle

Equator

macaw

Amazon River

SOUTH AMERICA

More than 5 billion people live in the world.

PACIFIC OCEAN

Driest place in the world.

condor

Atacama Desert

sperm whale

The great rainforests of the world help to create the air we need to breathe. The biggest is in Brazil, South America. There are others in Central America, Africa, Asia and Australia.

llama

SOUTHERN OCEAN

albatross

penguins

14

On land, the highest mountains are the Himalayas in Asia. Mount Everest is the highest peak.

There are great trenches under the oceans. The Marianas Trench in the Pacific is 10,911m deep.

The highest mountains on earth are under the sea. Mauna Loa is a mountain in the Pacific Ocean. Its peak sticks up out of the sea, forming an island. If it were uncovered, it would be higher than Mount Everest.

ARCTIC OCEAN

narwhal

wolf

bear

ASIA

reindeer

Biggest lake in the world.

giant panda

Highest place in the world.

PACIFIC OCEAN

Caspian Sea

Lowest place in the world.

snow leopard

Dead Sea

Mount Everest

Longest river in the world.

Deepest part of the oceans.

River Nile

Cherrapunji, India

Asian elephant

The Marianas Trench

Dalol, Ethiopia Hottest place in the world.

orangutan

great white shark

INDIAN OCEAN

Wettest place in the world.

dolphins

kangaroo

lemurs

The great rivers are the lifelines of the continents. They provide water and carry people and goods across countries.

platypus

AUSTRALASIA AND OCEANIA

kiwi

Coldest place in the world.

survey ship

fin whale

Asia is the biggest continent. The smallest is Australasia.

Plateau Station

ANTARCTICA

15

The Arctic

The Arctic is a frozen ocean, surrounded by land. An imaginary line called the Arctic Circle marks where it is.

Aleutian Islands

PACIFIC OCEAN

BERING SEA

ice-breaking ship

beluga whale

Sakh (Rus

Sea of Okhotsk

walrus

ALASKA (USA)

Arctic fox

CHUKCHI SEA

brown bear

Wrangel Island

Some of the ice in th Arctic melts in the summer, but it st stays very cold

CANADA

Arctic Circle

Arctic hare

dog sled

BEAUFORT SEA

stoa

musk ox

polar bear

New Siberian Islands

Laptev Sea

reindeer

Victoria Island

RUSSIA

igloo

Severnaya Zemlya

wolf

Ellesmere Island (Canada)

North Pole

kayak

Baffin Island

Franz Josef Land

Kara Sea

BAFFIN BAY

sn ov

GREENLAND

Novaya Zemlya

DAVIS STRAIT

hooded seal

skidoo

Svalbard (Norway)

narwhal

wolveri

grey seal

Barents Sea

raccoon dog

Arctic tern

Norwegian Sea

ATLANTIC OCEAN

16

hot springs

cod

ICELAND

sperm whale

The Inuit people live in the Arctic. They are skilled hunter and have found ways to survive the extreme cold.

Antarctica

Antarctica is the coldest place on earth.
It is land covered by ice and snow.
Hardly anything can survive there.

No people live in Antarctica all
the time, but there are a few
scientific bases set up by different
countries. Scientists visit the bases
to do experiments.

ATLANTIC OCEAN

albatross

survey ship

cod

elephant seal

SOUTHERN OCEAN

blue whale

South Orkney Islands (UK)

Weddell Sea

Queen Maud Land

tracked vehicle

gentoo penguin

weddell seal

skidoo

scientists

Amery Ice Shelf

Alexander Island

Ronne Ice Shelf

East Antarctica

rockhopper penguin

Ellsworth Mountains 4897m

South Pole

Queen Mary Land

blue-eyed shag

West Antarctica

polar aircraft

krill

Ross Ice Shelf

Wilkes Land

emperor penguin

leopard seal

Ross Sea

PACIFIC OCEAN

chinstrap penguin

Antarctic Circle

The lowest temperature ever recorded was in Antarctica. It was -89.2°C.

Scientists think that the ice on Antarctica is melting. If this happens, the world's oceans will get deeper and some of its land will be covered in water.

SOUTHERN OCEAN

fin whale

Canada

ARCTIC OCEAN

Canada is a very big country. It has many high mountains and is very cold in winter. Parts of Canada are inside the Arctic Circle.

Arctic char

Elle
Is

Queen Elizabeth Islands

ALASKA (USA)

Beaufort Sea

beluga whale

Banks Island

Prince of Wales Island

Arctic Circle

Mount McKinley

polar bear

Victoria Island

great northern diver

American black bear

Arctic hare

Great Bear Lake

muskrat

snow goose

skidoo

Whitehorse

Canada has lots of oil under the ground that no one has ever used.

grey whale

Mackenzie River

Yellowknife

Great Slave Lake

logging

woodchuck

Churc

totem pole

R o c k y   M o u n t a i n s

Lake Athabasca

Queen Charlotte Islands

mounted police

Reindeer Lake

beaver

Lake Winnipeg

salmon

Edmonton

North American porcupine

Lake Manitoba

Vancouver Island

Vancouver

Calgary

Regina

Lake Winnipeg

Victoria

wild turkey

PACIFIC OCEAN

monarch butterfly

sperm whale

The Rocky Mountains stretch down through the west of Canada.

UNITED STATES OF AMERICA

18

Greenland is the biggest island in the world. It belongs to Denmark. Hardly anyone lives there.

ICELAND

narwhal

Reykjavik

Iceland is part of Europe. It has lots of volcanoes and hot springs, called geysers.

Qaanaaq

harp seal

GREENLAND
(DENMARK)

Baffin Bay

Arctic Circle

herring

walrus

bowhead whale

razorbill

Baffin Island

Davis Strait

Nuuk

trawler

Foxe Basin

Canada is at the top of the North American continent. It is the second biggest country in the world.

cod

...uthampton Island

Hudson Strait

white-beaked dolphin

The English and French languages are both spoken in Canada.

...udson Bay

igloo

ATLANTIC OCEAN

kayak

Canada goose

Belcher Islands

CANADA

Newfoundland

St John's

St Lawrence River

Gulf of St Lawrence

Prince Edward Island

The Great Lakes are inland seas. They are joined to the Atlantic Ocean by the St Lawrence River.

Charlottetown

Fredericton

Halifax

Quebec

gannet

Nova Scotia

CN Tower

Montreal

N

Lake Superior

Ottawa

Toronto

W   E

killer whale

Lake Huron

Lake Ontario

Niagara Falls

Lake Michigan

S

Lake Erie

19

USA

The United States of America (USA) is divided into 50 states. There are mountains, forests, lakes, prairies and deserts in different parts of the USA.

killer whale

Seattle

Portland

giant redwood tree

red deer

wolf

bald eagle

Mount Rushmore

Golden Gate Bridge

mountain goat

bison

Salt Lake City

rattlesnake

UNITED STATES OF AMERICA

San Francisco
San José

Denver

CASINO

pronghorn

PACIFIC OCEAN

Death Valley

Las Vegas

Hollywood

HOLLYWOOD

Grand Canyon

Los Angeles

Colorado River

cactus

San Diego

beef cattle

Phoenix

Hawaii (USA)

surfing

rodeo

Alaska and Hawaii are part of the USA. Can you find them on the world map?

MEXICO

San Anton

RUSSIA

ALASKA (USA)

CANADA

fur seal

Mount McKinley

sea otter

The people who lived in America before it became the USA are called Native Americans. There are different Native American tribes, such as the Sioux and the Navaho.

People have come from all over the world to settle in the USA. The main languages are English and Spanish.

CANADA

N

W   E

S

Lake Superior

Lake Huron

Lake Ontario

Statue of Liberty

beaver

Boston

Minneapolis

raccoon

Lake Michigan

Lake Erie

Detroit

New York

humpback whale

Philadelphia

Chicago

Indianapolis

chipmunk

Washington DC

The Statue of Liberty in New York is known as a symbol of the USA worldwide.

The White House

Kansas City

St Louis

Appalachian Mountains

Charlotte

The capital city of America is Washington DC. The President lives there.

farming

skunk

Memphis

Atlanta

ATLANTIC OCEAN

Mississippi River

river boat

oranges

alligator

America is famous for exploring space. The first person ever to land on the Moon was Neil Armstrong in 1969. Rockets are launched from Cape Canaveral in Florida.

Dallas

New Orleans

Houston

Cape Canaveral

marlin

There are lots of hurricanes every year in the south and mid-west of America. Hurricane Katrina hit New Orleans in 2005. Parts of the city were destroyed by the strong winds and floods.

Miami

oil platform

GULF OF MEXICO

Disneyland

Central America and the West Indies

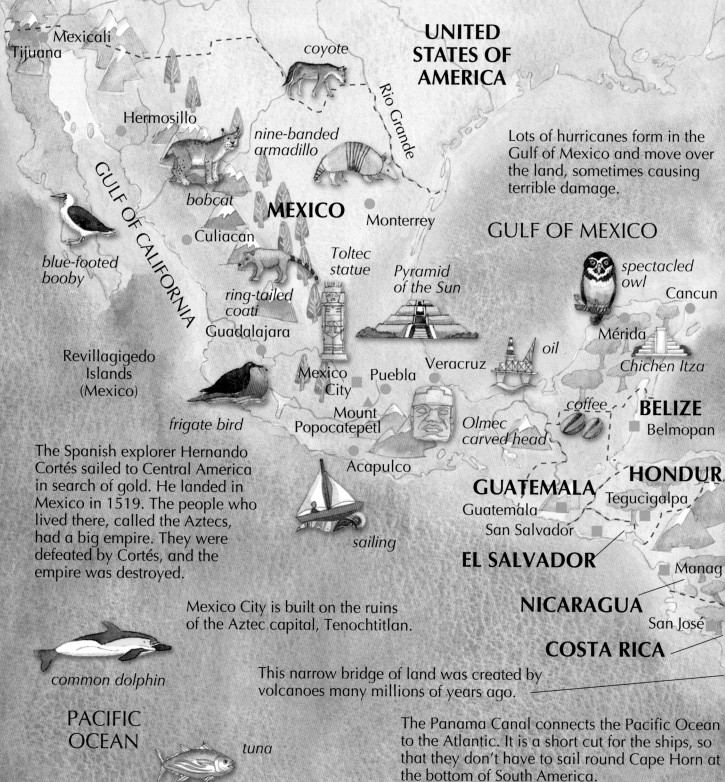

Mexicali
Tijuana

coyote

UNITED STATES OF AMERICA

Rio Grande

Hermosillo

nine-banded armadillo

Lots of hurricanes form in the Gulf of Mexico and move over the land, sometimes causing terrible damage.

bobcat

MEXICO

Monterrey

GULF OF MEXICO

GULF OF CALIFORNIA

Culiacan

Toltec statue

Pyramid of the Sun

spectacled owl

Cancun

blue-footed booby

ring-tailed coati

Mérida

Guadalajara

oil

Chichen Itza

Revillagigedo Islands (Mexico)

Veracruz

coffee

BELIZE

Belmopan

Mexico City

Puebla

frigate bird

Mount Popocatepetl

Olmec carved head

The Spanish explorer Hernando Cortés sailed to Central America in search of gold. He landed in Mexico in 1519. The people who lived there, called the Aztecs, had a big empire. They were defeated by Cortés, and the empire was destroyed.

Acapulco

HONDUR

GUATEMALA

Tegucigalpa

Guatemala

San Salvador

sailing

EL SALVADOR

Manag

Mexico City is built on the ruins of the Aztec capital, Tenochtitlan.

NICARAGUA

San José

COSTA RICA

common dolphin

This narrow bridge of land was created by volcanoes many millions of years ago.

PACIFIC OCEAN

The Panama Canal connects the Pacific Ocean to the Atlantic. It is a short cut for the ships, so that they don't have to sail round Cape Horn at the bottom of South America.

tuna

The Galapagos Islands have lots of unusual birds and animals. The biologist Charles Darwin, who first wrote that living things evolved (changed) over thousands of years, formed some of his ideas after visiting the islands.

giant tortoise

GALAPAGOS ISLANDS (ECUADOR)

iguana

There are thousands of islands that make up the West Indies. Many of them are tiny with few or no people. The islands are the tops of a mountain range that lies under the sea.

diving

cruise ship

sailfish

NORTH ATLANTIC OCEAN

Cuvier's beaked whale

BAHAMAS

■ Nassau

SAN SALVADOR

TURKS & CAICOS ISLANDS (UK)

PUERTO RICO (USA)

VIRGIN ISLANDS (UK & USA)

ANGUILLA (UK)

ST MARTIN (FRANCE)

sugar cane

Havana

CUBA

pirate wrecks

bee hummingbird (the world's smallest bird)

DOMINICAN REPUBLIC

HAITI

Port-au-Prince

Santo Domingo

San Juan

ANTIGUA & BARBUDA

GUADELOUPE (FRANCE)

JAMAICA

■ Kingston

ST KITTS & NEVIS

MONTSERRAT (UK)

DOMINICA

CAYMAN ISLANDS (UK)

CARIBBEAN SEA

MARTINIQUE (FRANCE)

ST VINCENT & THE GRENADINES

ST LUCIA

BARBADOS

tarpon

brown pelican

Port of Spain

GRENADA

TRINIDAD & TOBAGO

Panama Canal

flamingo

PANAMA

River Orinoco

bananas

Panama City

sun parakeet

LF OF NAMA

Christopher Columbus sailed west from Europe. He was trying to find an easier route to the rich countries of the east. He landed on San Salvador, in the Bahamas, in 1492, and thought he had found India. This is why the islands were called the West Indies.

N

W E

S

South America

South America covers a huge area. It has mountains, rainforests and grassy plains, called pampas, that stretch for miles.

The main languages spoken in South America are Spanish, Portuguese and English.

CARIBBEAN SEA

ATLANTIC OCEAN

The Amazon River is the second longest river in the world.

oil tanker

oil platform

Maracaibo

Caracas

VENEZUELA

armadillo

Medellin

Bogotá

COLOMBIA

Quito

Mount Cotopaxi

spectacled bear

ECUADOR

cruise ship

GUYANA

Georgetown

SURINAME

Paramaribo

Angel Falls (world's highest waterfall)

French rocket base

Cayenne

FRENCH GUIANA

piranha fish

capybara

Manaus

River Amazon

Belem

toucan

sloth

giant anteater

squirrel monkey

Amazon river dolphin

anaconda

jaguar

scarlet macaw

BRAZIL

Brasilia

manatee

Equator

Fortaleza

Cape of Sao Roque

Recife

scarlet ibis

Salvador

Machupicchu ruins

Lima

alpaca

PERU

Lake Titicaca

Mount Ancohuma

La Paz

BOLIVIA

Lake Titicaca is the highest lake in the world. It is 3,812m

24

ATLANTIC OCEAN

bottlenose dolphin

ocelot

● Rio de Janeiro

● São Paulo

Statue of Christ in Rio de Janeiro

● Pôrto Alegre

The rainforest in Brazil is the biggest one in the world. It is so thick in places that the sunlight does not reach the forest floor. It rains every day and sometimes the Amazon river floods.

Trees in the rainforest help to make the air we breathe. In places, however, the trees have been cut down to make room for growing crops. If the rainforest disappears it is likely to affect the planet's climate.

blue whale

South Georgia (UK)

The tip of South America is near Antarctica. It is very cold.

mail ship

albatross

fin whale

PARAGUAY

Asunción ■

falabella mini horse

URUGUAY

Montevideo ■

River Plate

vampire bat

beef cattle

The Atacama Desert is the driest place on Earth.

chinchilla

Mount Aconcagua ■

Buenos Aires

ARGENTINA

CHILE

llama

shellfish

Santiago ■

sheep

puma

Falkland Islands (UK)

● Stanley

leopard seal

Tierra del Fuego

A n d e s

Risso's dolphin

sardines

volcanoes

Cape Horn

elephant seal

The sea around Cape Horn is a very dangerous place for ships. It has strong currents and violent storms.

SOUTHERN OCEAN

PACIFIC OCEAN

The Incas lived in Peru hundreds of years ago. They built an empire which stretched over Chile and Ecuador. The Incas worshipped the sun and nature gods. Lots of people visit the ruins of Machupicchu, one of the cities where the Incas lived.

The Andes is the longest mountain range in the world. Some people live high in the mountains. They use llamas to carry loads up the narrow mountain paths.

N

E

W

S

Western Europe

Europe is made up of lots of different countries. In the past, European countries controlled many lands far away from Europe. They still govern some faraway islands, called 'territories'.

Parts of Europe in the far north are very cold. The upper areas of Norway, Sweden and Finland are all inside the Arctic Circle.

A warm ocean current called the Gulf Stream runs from North America, past Europe and into the Arctic Circle. If it wasn't there, the sea around northern Europe would be much colder and the winters longer and harder.

Much of Europe has a mild climate, which means the weather is not extremely hot or cold all the time.

ICELAND

Reykjavik

Arctic Circle

eider duck

ATLANTIC OCEAN

fishing boat

Faroe Islands
(Denmark)

Rockall (UK)

Shetland Islands
(UK)

Western Isles
(UK)

golden eagle

Orkney Islands
(UK)

cattle

Northern Ireland
(UK)

IRELAND

Dublin

Belfast

basking shark

Birmingham
Cardiff

Liverpool

Glasgow
Edinburgh

Aberdeen

UNITED KINGDOM

cod

Norwegian Sea

cuckoo wrasse

puffin

North Sea

Trondheim

NORWAY

stavekirk

Bergen

Oslo

SWEDEN

Gulf of Bothnia

snowy owl

Narvik

Tromso

Hammerfest

Kiruna

reindeer

FINLAND

Helsinki

Tallinn

ESTONIA

Uppsala

Stockholm

Lake Vanern

Gothenburg

Gotland

Riga

LATVIA

LITHUANIA

Vilnius

Part of RUSSIA

Kaliningrad

POLAND

Gdansk

historic ships

DENMARK

Copenhagen
Malmo
Baltic Sea

ferry

NETHERLANDS

Hamburg

Brandenburg

Tower Bridge

CZECH REP. · Prague · Black Forest · Munich

SLOVAKIA · Krakow · Bratislava

AUSTRIA · Vienna · Salzburg

HUNGARY · Budapest

SLOVENIA · Ljubljana

River Danube · Zagreb · Belgrade

CROATIA · Sarajevo

BOSNIA-HERZEGOVINA

SERBIA · Podgorica

MONTE-NEGRO · Tirana

SKopje · *olive tree* · GREECE · Athens

ALBANIA · MACEDONIA

Mount Vesuvius · Mount Etna

ITALY · Colosseum · Rome · Naples · *olive tree*

Sicily (Italy) · MALTA · Valletta

seahorse · *trumpetfish*

The Mediterranean Sea is warm and quite shallow. It only has a narrow channel connecting it to the Atlantic Ocean. Because of this, it has hardly any tides at all.

LUXEMBOURG · LIECHTENSTEIN · *grapes*

SWITZERLAND · Bern · Alps · Venice · *gondola*

ITALY · Leaning Tower of Pisa · SAN MARINO

Milan · Corsica (France) · Sardinia (Italy) · Cagliari · *octopus*

FRANCE · Lyons · Mont Blanc · *wild horses* · Marseilles

Eiffel Tower · Paris

Southern European countries are very hot in the summer.

NORTH AFRICA

grapes · River Loire · Nantes · ANDORRA · Pyrenees · River Garonne · Barcelona

Balearic Islands · Minorca · Majorca (Spain) · Ibiza · Mediterranean Sea

anchovies

Bay of Biscay · Bordeaux · Bilbao · Pamplona · Madrid · SPAIN · *flamenco dancers* · Granada

cruise ship · *pilchards* · Vigo · Oporto · *olive tree* · PORTUGAL · Lisbon · River Tagus · Cordoba · Malaga · Gibraltar (UK) · Ceuta (Spain)

bulls

Most countries in Europe are part of a group called the European Union. Some of these countries now use the same currency (money) called the Euro.

N · E · W · S

27

Eastern Europe

This part of Europe contains many countries. In the far north the climate is very cold. Down in the south the climate is much warmer.

Arctic Circle

Barents Sea

ice-breaking ship

Murmansk

White Sea

Arkhangelsk

Arctic fox

Hammerfest

reindeer

NORWAY

snowy owl

Sami reindeer herders

SWEDEN

mountain hare

Uppsala

Stockholm

Lake Vänern

Malmo

Gulf of Bothnia

FINLAND

Vaasa

Tampere

Helsinki

Gulf of Finland

Tallinn

ESTONIA

Gotland

historic ships

Baltic Sea

LATVIA

Riga

LITHUANIA

Vilnius

RUSSIA

Kaliningrad

elk

brown bear

grey wolf

Ural Mountains

osprey

Lake Onega

Lake Ladoga

St Petersburg

Winter Palace

RUSSIA

badger

Smolensk

BELARUS

In 1917, there was a revolution in Russia and the king (called the Tsar) and his family were killed. The country was ruled by the communist party until 1991. It now has an elected President.

River Volga

St Basil's Cathedral

Moscow

The Volga is Europe's longest river.

River Volga

One of the world's worst nuclear accidents happened at Chernobyl, in the Ukraine, in 1986. Radioactive material

28

Some European countries were ruled by Soviet Russia for many years. All are now independent.

Cossack dancers Volgograd

River Volga

Caspian Sea

AZERBAIJAN

oil

otter

Caucasus Mountains

Tbilisi

GEORGIA

ARMENIA

Yerevan

Trabzon

grapes

Lake Van

SYRIA

Damascus

cotton

red deer

Samsun

Ankara

TURKEY

Adana

Taurus Mountains

Konya

CYPRUS
(Greece, Turkey)

Nicosia

Cyprus has been split into two parts since a war in the 1960s. The North is ruled by people loyal to Turkey and the south is ruled by people loyal to Greece.

Chernobyl

Kiev

UKREINE

Donetsk

River Dnieper

wild boar

Crimea

Black Sea

Odesa

Chisinau

MOLDOVA

Sevastopol

The Bosphorus and Dardanelles link the Black Sea to the Mediterranean.

sturgeon

The Bosphorus

Hagia Sofia

Istanbul

The Dardanelles

Izmir

olive tree

Rhodes
(Greece)

Iraklion

Crete
(Greece)

oil

Transylvanian Alps

grapes

Prague

CZECH REP.

SLOVAKIA

Vlad Dracul's castle

Lvov

Krakow

ROMANIA

Bucharest

River Danube

Sofia

BULGARIA

Skopje

Thessaloniki

olive tree

GREECE

Athens

Parthenon

Vienna

Bratislava

Budapest

AUSTRIA

HUNGARY

SLOVENIA

Ljubljana

Zagreb

CROATIA

Belgrade

SERBIA

Sarajevo

BOSNIA-
HERZEGOVINA

Podgorica

MONTENEGRO

Tirana

ALBANIA

MACEDONIA

ITALY

Mediterranean Sea

N
E
S
W

29

Eurasia

Eurasia includes parts of Europe and Asia. Russia stretches right across it, and is the biggest country in the world.

Franz Josef (Russia

ARCTIC OCEAN

Barents Sea

harp seal

Murmansk

Kola Peninsula

arctic char

Novaya Zemlya (Russia)

FINLAND

Helsinki

Arctic Circle

Kara Sea

wild boar

St Petersburg

WHITE SEA

Arkhangelsk

eider duck

lemming

Minsk

BELARUS

St Basil's Cathedral

white-tailed eagle

Kiev

UKRAINE

Moscow

RUSSIA

Nizhniy Novgorod

River Ob

West of the Ural Mountains, Russia is considered to be in Europe. East of the Urals, it is in Asia.

Donetsk

wheat harvest

Kazan

Perm

Ural Mountains

osprey

Rostov

River Volga

Samara

Ufa

Yekaterinburg

Chelyabinsk

Russia has vast areas of open grassland called steppe.

Volgograd

flamingo

Mount Elbrus

ibex

Omsk

Tomsk

GEORGIA

Atyrau

Astrakhan

saiga

Novosibirs

Tbilisi

sturgeon

oil

Aral Sea

KAZAKHSTAN

Yerevan

Actau

Baikonur Cosmodrome

Astana

yak

Baku

Caspian Sea

white pelican

Qaraghandy

AZERBAIJAN

cotton

A cosmodrome is a space rocket launch site. A cosmonaut is the Russian word for an astronaut.

Lake Balkhash

ARMENIA

Tehran

TURKMENISTAN

UZBEKISTAN

TAJIKISTAN

Almaty

CHINA

IRAN

Ashgabat

Tashkent

Samarkand

Bishkek

KYRGYZSTAN

Urumqi

N

W E

S

Dashanbe

Some of the smaller countries below Russia, such as Kazakhstan and Turkmenistan, were part of the Soviet Union until the early 1990s, when they became independent. The Soviet Union was ruled by Russia.

Wrangel Island (Russia)

Arctic Circle

right whale

Severnaya Zemlya (Russia)

New Siberian Islands (Russia)

arctic fox

Taymyr Peninsula

Laptev Sea

snowy owl

walrus

sable

reindeer

River Lena

Kamchatka Peninsula

Magadan

pika

volcanoes

elk

Petropavlovsk-Kamchatskiy

raccoon dog

oil

Siberia, in Russia, has vast areas of forest called taiga.

sea otter

Sea of Okhotsk

Kuril Islands (Russia)

brown bear

Sakhalin (Russia)

Lake Baikal is 1,741m deep. It is the deepest lake in the world and contains one fifth of the world's fresh water.

The Trans-Siberian railway goes from Moscow to Vladivostok, a distance of 9,311km.

RUSSIA

Bratsk

Eurasian lynx

Khabarovsk

Lake Baikal

Chita

Siberian tiger

Japanese crane

Irkutsk

Ulan Ude

Qiqihar

Vladivostok

Ulan Bator

Harbin

Sea of Japan

JAPAN

MONGOLIA

ger

CHINA

Shenyang

giant octopus

dhole

long-eared jerboa

Tokyo

Beijing

31

Middle East and Western Asia

LEBANON

Beirut

SYRIA

golden hamster

ISRAEL

Damascus

UZBEKIST

Baku

oil

oil

oil

Caspian Sea

TURKMENISTAN

Sama

Ashgabat

Jerusalem

Gaza City

Amman

JORDAN

IRAQ

mosque

Tehran

Mashhad

Herat

Dead Sea

Baghdad

ziggurat

Esfahan

caracal

IRAN

AFGHANISTA

West Bank and Gaza Strip
(PALESTINIAN AUTHORITY)

The shores of the Dead Sea are the lowest land in the world.

oil

Basra

Abadan

Kuwait

Shiraz

Kerman

Zahedan

EGYPT

kestrel

Medina

SAUDI ARABIA

KUWAIT

BAHRAIN

honey badger

PAKIST

Red Sea

Riyadh

Manama

QATAR

oil

Jeddah

the Ka'ba

Doha

oil

Dubai

Mecca

The holy city of Mecca is in Saudi Arabia. Muslims all over the world turn towards Mecca to pray.

Abu Dhabi

Kar

cruise ship

Bedouin tent

UNITED ARAB EMIRATES

oil

Muscat

OMAN

oil tanker

camels

oil

Arabian Sea

Sana

vulturine guineafowl

YEMEN

manta ray

The ruins of the ancient civilization of Babylon are in Iraq.

Aden

arab dhow

Socotra
(Yemen)

The Indian Ocean is the third largest ocean, after the Pacific and the Atlantic.

butterfly fish

N

Bedouin Arabs live in the deserts of the Middle East. They move from place to place to find food and water for themselves and their animals.

W   E

S

INDIAN OCEAN

The countries on the left of this page form a part of Asia called the Middle East. Many countries here are hot and dry, and it is difficult to grow things. Many Middle Eastern countries produce oil which is used in the rest of the world.

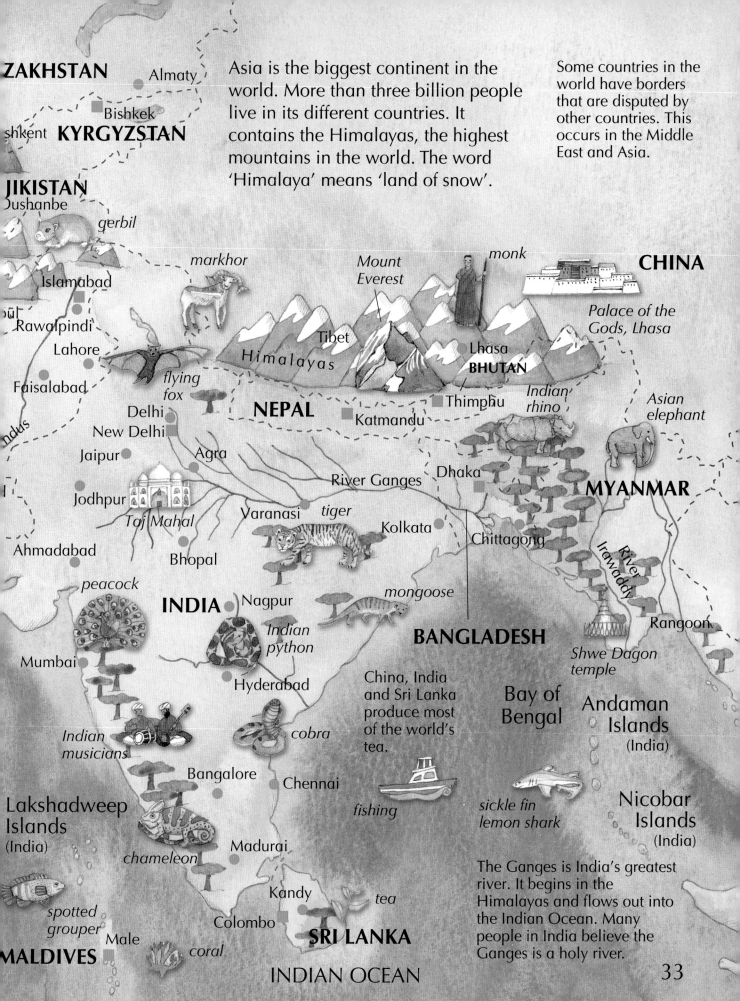

ZAKHSTAN

Almaty

Bishkek

shkent **KYRGYZSTAN**

JIKISTAN

Dushanbe

gerbil

markhor

Islamabad

monk

Mount Everest

CHINA

Palace of the Gods, Lhasa

Asia is the biggest continent in the world. More than three billion people live in its different countries. It contains the Himalayas, the highest mountains in the world. The word 'Himalaya' means 'land of snow'.

Some countries in the world have borders that are disputed by other countries. This occurs in the Middle East and Asia.

ul

Rawalpindi

Lahore

Tibet

Lhasa

BHUTAN

flying fox

H i m a l a y a s

Faisalabad

Indian rhino

Asian elephant

ndus

Delhi

New Delhi

NEPAL

Thimphu

Jaipur

Agra

Katmandu

Jodhpur

River Ganges

Dhaka

MYANMAR

Taj Mahal

Varanasi

tiger

Kolkata

Chittagong

River Irawaddy

Ahmadabad

Bhopal

peacock

INDIA

Nagpur

mongoose

BANGLADESH

Rangoon

Shwe Dagon temple

Mumbai

Indian python

Hyderabad

China, India and Sri Lanka produce most of the world's tea.

Bay of Bengal

Andaman Islands

(India)

Indian musicians

cobra

Bangalore

Chennai

fishing

sickle fin lemon shark

Nicobar Islands

(India)

Lakshadweep Islands

(India)

chameleon

Madurai

The Ganges is India's greatest river. It begins in the Himalayas and flows out into the Indian Ocean. Many people in India believe the Ganges is a holy river.

spotted grouper

Kandy

tea

Male

coral

Colombo

SRI LANKA

MALDIVES

INDIAN OCEAN

33

South East Asia

China is part of South East Asia along with many island nations. Over a billion people live in China, more than in any other country in the world.

The Huang Ho (Yellow River) and the Yangtze Kiang are the two great rivers of China. They have been used for hundreds of years to transport people and goods all over the country.

The Great Wall of China was built more than two thousand years ago. It is 2,400km long.

Japan is a group of long narrow islands. Its highest mountain is the volcano, Mount Fuji.

KAZAKHSTAN

otter

Almaty

RUSSIA

muskrat

Urumqi

wild horses

Hotan

snow leopard

NEPAL

BANGLADESH

Katmandu

Dhaka

BHUTAN

Thimphu

INDIA

Kolkata

Irkutsk

MONGOLIA

Ulan Bator

mountain hare

Gobi Desert

silk moth

CHINA

Baotou

Great Wall of China

lesser panda

giant panda

Chinese space centre

Chongqing

Guiyang

Kunming

Guangzhou

Ulan Ude

Lake Baikal seal

Temple of Heaven

Beijing

Tianjin

Terracotta Army

Huang Ho

golden pheasant

Wuhan

Yangtze Kiang

Taipei

River Amur

Siberian tiger

Qiqihar

Harbin

Changchun

Shenyang

Khabarovsk

Vladivostock

NORTH KOREA

Pyongyang

Seoul

SOUTH KOREA

Nagasaki

Hiroshima

Shanghai

Sakhalin (Russia)

Sapporo

bullet train

Mount Fuji

Tokyo

Kobe

Kyoto

Osaka

JAPAN

traditional dress

tiger shark

Taipei 101 in Taiwan is the tallest occupied building in

Mariana Islands (USA)

PACIFIC OCEAN

puffer fish

angel fish

green turtle

Equator

PALAU

Koror

mudskipper

New Guinea

bird of paradise

lion fish

AUSTRALIA

Hong Kong is a tiny, overcrowded island off the coast of China. It was ruled by Britain until 1997, when it became part of China. Lots of people from all over the world live and work here, making it an interesting mix of east and west.

PHILIPPINES

Manila

Davao

flying lemur

orangutan

Celebes

Ambon

dugong

EAST TIMOR

komodo dragon

INDONESIA

praying mantis

sea dragon

South-east Asian countries manufacture clothes and other goods for countries around the world.

South China Sea

VIETNAM
LAOS
CAMBODIA

Ho Chi Minh City

Phnom Penh

Angkor Wat

BRUNEI

Bandar Seri Begawan

Borneo

proboscis monkey

Surabaya

Bandung

Java

Christmas Island (Australia)

There are thousands of islands off the tip of Asia. Many of them make up countries such as the Philippines and Indonesia. There are over 3,000 islands in Indonesia.

THAILAND

Bangkok

Gulf of Thailand

MALAYSIA

Kuala Lumpur

Singapore

Sumatra

Jakarta

Medan

Malayan tapir

Javan rhino

killer whale

Cocos Islands (Australia)

Bengal Rangoon

Andaman Islands (India)

slow loris

Nicobar Islands (India)

tarantula spider

INDIAN OCEAN

The monsoon is a wind that starts in the Indian Ocean and brings very heavy rain to parts of southern Asia during the rainy season. Very little rain falls at other times of the year.

N
E
S
W

35

North Africa

N
W E
S

Southern Europe

sardines

Tangier

Oran

Algiers

Tunis

TUNISIA

date palms

Fès

Rabat

Casablanca

MOROCCO

Marrakech

Atlas Mountains

Agadir

Funchal

Madeira (Portugal)

Canary Islands (Spain)

Las Palmas

Santa Cruz de Tenerife

Laayoune

WESTERN SAHARA

sun fish

underground houses

Tripoli

oil

The Sahara is the biggest desert in the world. The highest temperature ever was recorded here (57.7° C). Wandering tribes called nomads live here.

●In Salah

ALGERIA

fennec fox

MAURITANIA

Sahara Desert

mud-brick buildings

camels

caracal

Nouakchott

flamingo

spotted hyena

Timbouctou

River Niger

NIGER

●Agadèz

River Senegal

Dakar

SENEGAL

Banjul

Bissau

MALI

Bamako

BURKINA FASO

Niamey

Kano

Ndjame

Maiduguri

GUINEA

Conakry

Ouagadougou

BENIN

gold and diamonds

pygmy hippo

Lake Volta

NIGERIA

Abuja

Ibadan

leopard

GUINEA BISSAU

Freetown

Monrovia

IVORY COAST

Abidjan

Accra

Lagos

Porto Novo

Lomé

Port Harcourt

CAMEROON

GAMBIA

SIERRA LEONE

LIBERIA

GHANA

TOGO

oil

Yaoundé

Africa is the second biggest continent in the world. It is made up of 53 countries. It has vast deserts, mountains, savanna (grasslands) and rainforests. Many parts of Africa are hot and dry, making it difficult to grow food.

EQUATORIAL GUINEA

Libreville

CONGO

GABON

Brazza

The Nile is the longest river in the world (6,690km). It flows north through Egypt. The great civilization of Ancient Egypt was built on the banks of the Nile.

The Suez Canal was built to join the Red Sea to the Mediterranean. It is 160km long.

There are many languages spoken in Africa. In the countries north of the Sahara, Arabic is spoken. Further south, many Africans speak French or English as well as their own languages.

Lots of animals live on the great grasslands of Africa. Many were once hunted for their skins until they were in danger of dying out. There are now huge game reserves to help protect them.

There are enormous rainforests in the central part of Africa.

albacore

hazi

Mediterranean Sea

Suez Canal

Port Said

Alexandria

oil

EGYPT

Suez

Cairo

LIBYA

pyramids

Egyptian vulture

scorpion

Sahara Desert

Lake Nasser

Red Sea

Sudan is the biggest African country.

HAD

cheetah

crocodile

Port Sudan

River Nile

ERITREA

SUDAN

Khartoum

Asmera

rock cut church

hants

El Obeid

ostrich

obelisk

DJIBOUTI

Gulf of Aden

scimitar horned oryx

serval

Djibouti

Hargeisa

Burao

kob

marabou stork

Addis Ababa

ETHIOPIA

CENTRAL AFRICAN REPUBLIC

SOMALI REPUBLIC

ETHIOPIAN HIGHLANDS

warthog

giraffe

ghi **Democratic Republic of the CONGO**

okapi

Lake Turkana

Mogadishu

INDIAN OCEAN

River Congo

UGANDA

KENYA

RWANDA

Kampala

coffee

Equator

sacred ibis

Nairobi

Mount Kilimanjaro (5,895m) – in Kenya and Tanzania

impanzee

Lake Victoria

zebra

37

Southern Africa

Much of Southern Africa is high, flat grassland. There are also deserts and mountains, and large deposits of gold, diamonds, copper and tin.

The Zaire River is one of the longest in the world. It flows through thick jungle and is a highway for the people who live in central Africa.

Many African countries used to be run by European countries. Now most are independent, which means they run themselves.

ATLANTIC OCEAN

There are water holes in the hot dry grasslands of Africa. Without these, the people and animals who live there would not survive.

Parts of central and southern Africa were first charted by the Scottish explorer, David Livingstone. He was the first outsider to discover the Victoria Falls. He died on his travels in 1873.

Nelson Mandela fought for the rights of black people in South Africa. After spending 28 years in prison on Robben Island, he became the country's first freely elected president in 1994.

The tip of Africa is called the Cape of Good Hope. It is one of the most dangerous shipping routes in the world.

38

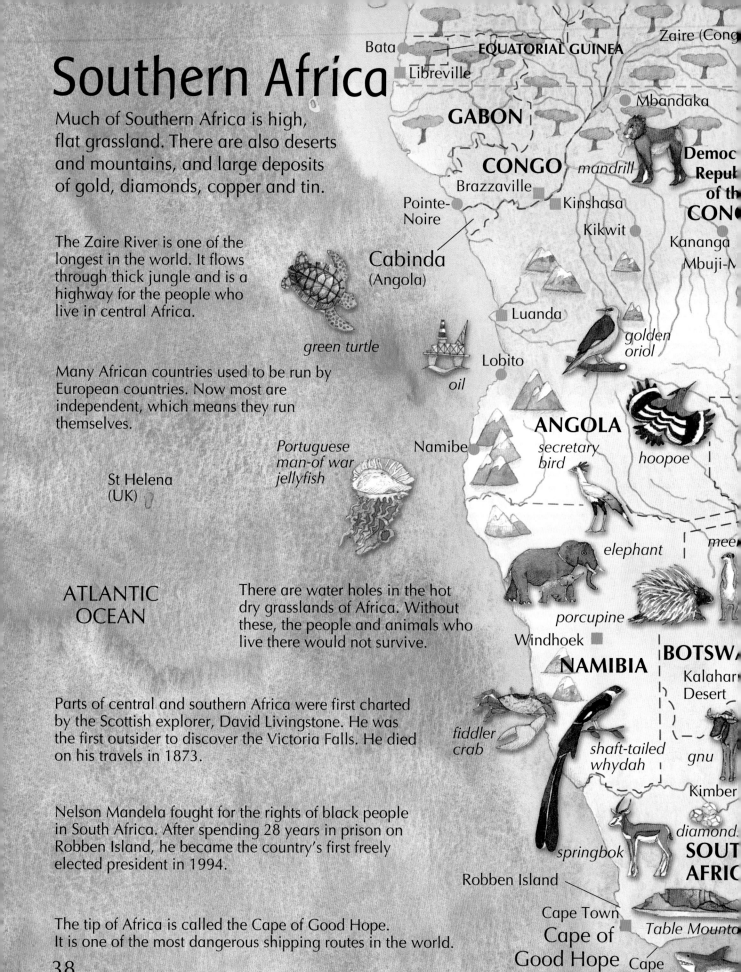

Bata
Libreville
EQUATORIAL GUINEA
Zaire (Cong
Mbandaka
GABON
mandrill
Democ
Repub
of th
CON
CONGO
Brazzaville
Kinshasa
Pointe-Noire
Kikwit
Kananga
Mbuji-M
Cabinda (Angola)
green turtle
Luanda
golden oriol
oil
Lobito
ANGOLA
secretary bird
hoopoe
Namibe
Portuguese man-of war jellyfish
St Helena (UK)
elephant
mee
porcupine
Windhoek
BOTSWA
NAMIBIA
Kalahar Desert
fiddler crab
shaft-tailed whydah
gnu
Kimber
diamond.
springbok
SOUT
AFRIC
Robben Island
Cape Town
Table Mounta
Cape of Good Hope
Cape Agulhas
great white

UGANDA

gorilla

Kampala

KENYA

SOMALIA

Mogadishu

Equator

Nairobi

Mount
Kilimanjaro
(5,895m)

Lake Victoria is the
world's second largest
freshwater lake,
measuring 67,850sq km.

SEYCHELLES

VANDA

Kigali

Lake
Victoria

Victoria

Bujumbura

Mombasa

BURUNDI

rhino

Kilimanjaro
partly in Tanzania

Zanzibar

Lake
Tanganyika

Dodoma

giraffe

Dar es Salaam

Aldabra
Islands
(Seychelles)

INDIAN
OCEAN

shoebill

hippo

rhino

Union of
COMOROS

ture

lion

TANZANIA

Moroni

Antsiranana

Ambilobe

Lake
Nyasa

fruit bat

Mayotte
(France)

sunbird asity

MBIA

MALAWI

Nacala

Mahajanga

aka

Lilongwe

Toamasina

ngstone

Blantyre

*baobab
tree*

Antananarivo

ZIMBABWE

lion

MADAGASCAR

Victoria
Falls

Harare

MAURITIUS

awayo

Beira

Port Louis

Great
Zimbabwe
ruins

kudu

Morombe

St Denis

goling

Réunion
(France)

aborone

MOZAMBIQUE

Toliara

Madagascar is one of the biggest
islands in the world. It is the only
place, apart from the Comoros,
where lemurs live in the wild.

Pretoria

*ring-tailed
lemur*

eto

Maputo

The Victoria Falls is the
world's widest waterfall,
at roughly 1.7km wide.
Local people call it
'mosi-oa-tunya', meaning
'the smoke that thunders'.

Johannesburg

Mbabane

SWAZILAND

Maseru

Durban

LESOTHO

Bloemfontein

gold

N

There are many different native
African peoples and many
languages. For instance, the
Zulus and the Xhosa people live
in South Africa. The Xhosa
people use tongue clicks as part
of their language.

manta ray

East London

rt Elizabeth

fin whale

W

E

39

S

Zambezi River

MOZAMBIQUE CHANNEL

Australasia and Oceania

The sea over the Marianas Trench is the deepest in the world.

Northern Mariana Islands (USA)

Saipan

Guam

Truk Atoll

Po

PALAU
Koror

lion fish

FEDERATED STATES OF MICRONESI

Equator

rainbow lorikeet

New Guinea

PAPUA NEW GUINEA

cassowary

Port Moresby

Honi

sea dragon

INDIAN OCEAN

Timor Sea

Gulf of Carpentaria

Darwin

butterfly fish

Coral Sea

Cairns

Great Barrier Reef

blue damse

Australasia is the smallest continent in the world. It includes Australia, New Zealand and many other island nations.

emu

Dampier

Great Sandy Desert

sulphur-crested cockatoo

AUSTRALIA

aborigine

Mount Isa

Alice Springs

koala

frilled lizard

Uluru

Brisbane

cora

Kalgoorlie-Boulder

Great Victoria Desert

Simpson Desert

Lord Ho Island (Australi

Perth

kangaroo

Broken Hill

Sydney Opera House

Fremantle

Adelaide

Canberra

Sydney

surfing

Uluru (also called Ayers Rock) is the biggest single rock in the world. It is marked with ancient paintings and carvings, made by the Aborigines, the first people in Australia.

Great Australian Bight

wombat

platypus

Tasm Sea

Melbourne

Tasmanian devil

Tasmania

Hobart

humpback whale

The desert of northern Australia is often called the 'Outback'. It is a difficult place to live, as there is very little food or water to find.

great white shark

The Great Barrier Reef stretches for 2,012km in shallow sea off the coast of Australia. It is made of coral with beautiful patterns and colours. The coral was produce tiny creatures called coral polyps. Lots of sea creatures live on the reef.

Gilbert
Islands

Micronesia is
made up of 607
small islands.

An atoll is a group of
islands around an area
of shallow water.
They are made from
coral which has grown
around underwater
volcanoes.

Honolulu

Hawaii (USA)

*Hawaiian
Dancer*

There are thousands of tiny islands
in the Pacific near Australia. Many
island groups are now independent,
but some still belong to the USA,
Britain, France or other countries.

Bikini Atoll

Marshall
Islands

Majuro

Bairiki

manta ray

bottlenose dolphin

PACIFIC
OCEAN

uru

KIRIBATI

Tokelau
(NZ)

American
Samoa
(USA)

cruise ship

Equator

barracuda

omon
ands

Fongafale

TUVALU

SAMOA

Marquesas
Islands

clown fish

VANUATU
rt-Vila

Wallis &
Futuna
(France)

Apia

Cook
Islands
(NZ)

FRENCH
POLYNESIA
(France)

Suva

TONGA

Society
Islands

Papeete

FIJI

Nuku'alofa

Niue
(NZ)

Tahiti

bananas

New Caledonia (France)

Noumea

Kermadec Islands
(NZ)

*parrot
fish*

flying fish

Kingston

Norfolk Island
(Australia)

Some Pacific islands
are so densely covered
in trees that no humans
have ever lived there.

octopus

Pitcairn
Islands
(UK)

Auckland

NEW
EALAND

i

geyser

Maori

Wellington

Christchurch

sheep

Dunedin

Stewart Island

New Zealand has two
main islands – North
and South Island. There
are lots of volcanoes on
North Island, along
with hot water springs
called geysers.

Chatham Islands (New Zealand)

Bounty Islands (New Zealand)

Antipodes Islands (New Zealand)

Auckland Islands (New Zealand)

Campbell Island (New Zealand)

yacht

container ship

albatross

blue whale

sperm whale

The Exploring Game

Imagine you are an explorer travelling the world looking for amazing creatures and places. Whenever you want to play the exploring game, pick some pictures shown below and search for them on the maps in this book. Find the answers on page 45.

Two orangutans

Two kiwi birds

Two igloos

Four albatross birds

An alligator

A chipmunk

A totem pole

A spectacled owl

An iguana

A pirate flag

A manatee

Two leopard seals

Three great white sharks

Four blue whales

Two octopuses

A bull chasing
a man

A golden eagle

Two sturgeon
fishes

A Cossack dancer

A saiga

A sunfish

A zebra

A spotted hyena

A pair of
meerkats

A flying fox

A chameleon

A puffer fish

A tarantula
spider

A koala bear

Two sea
dragons

Glossary

Antarctic Circle
An imaginary circle drawn around the far south of the world.

Arctic Circle
An imaginary circle drawn around the far north of the world.

Atmosphere
A layer of air wrapped around the world. It contains the oxygen we need to breathe.

Capital city
The main city in a country, where the government of the country has its base.

Compass (on a map)
A symbol on a map, marked with the directions of north, south, east and west.

Continent
The seven main areas of land in the world – North America, South America, Europe, Asia, Australasia, Africa and Antarctica.

Core
The centre of the Earth, made up of incredibly hot metal and rock.

Country
An area of land that has its own government, citizens and boundaries.

Crust
A layer of rock around the surface of the Earth.

Current
Water flowing in one direction, in an ocean or a river.

Desert
An area of land where there is very little or no water.

Earthquake
When two of the Earth's plates move slightly against each other. This causes the Earth's surface to shudder and sometimes to split.

Equator
An imaginary line around the middle of the Earth.

Grassland
An area of land where most of the plants are grass.

Hurricane
A strong wind that can do lots of damage.

Magma

Molten (very hot) rock beneath the Earth's crust. Sometimes magma comes up to the surface through volcanoes.

Mantle

A layer beneath the Earth's crust, made up of magma (very hot rock).

Monsoon

A wind that blows across Asia at certain times of the year, bringing heavy rains.

North Pole

The point at the far north of the Earth.

Plates

Giant pieces of rock that make up the Earth's crust. They fit together rather like a jigsaw.

Rainforest

A jungle in an area of the world where there is lots of rainfall and hot weather.

South Pole

The point at the far south of the Earth.

Tundra

An area of land where it is so cold that few plants can grow. Tundra is found near the Arctic and Antarctic Circles.

WEBLINKS

Parragon does not accept responsibility for the content of any websites mentioned in this publication. If you have any queries about their content, please refer to the organization that produced the website. If you are under 18, the websites mentioned should only be used with the involvement of a parent or guardian.

http://www.bbc.co.uk/nature/animals/
Includes live webcams from around the world, with lots of animal features, quizzes and activities.

http://www.earthcamforkids.com
See lots of images from live webcams all over the world, including famous places, animals and space.

http://www.earth.nasa.gov/
A site run by space experts NASA. You can see lots of up-to-the-minute satellite pictures of Earth beamed from space.

http://www.nationalgeographic.com
National Geographic have a kids' section on their website, which includes games and facts about the Earth. Try out their amazing map machine, too. Click on 'kids' in the site index.

Answers to game: Orangutans p15, 35. Kiwi birds p15, 41. Igloos p16,19. Albatrosses p14, 17, 25, 41. Totem pole p18. Alligator p21, Chipmunk p21, Spectacled owl p22, Iguana p22, Pirate flag p23. Manatee p24, Leopard seals p17, 25. Great White Sharks p15, 38, 40. Blue whales p14, 17, 25, 41. Octopuses p27, 31. Bull chasing a man p27. Golden eagle p26. Sturgeons p29, 30. Cossack dancer p29. Saiga p30. Sun fish p36. Zebra p37. Spotted hyena p36. Meercats p38. Flying fox p33. Chameleon p33. Puffer fish p35. Sea dragons p35, 40. Tarantula spider p35. Koala bear p40.

Index